No Matter What

WRITTEN BY
Adrienne E. Anzelmo

ILLUSTRATED BY
Jessica M. Charpentier

To my children,
for showing me life and love through
a different lens.
   -A.E.A

To W.C.C..
May I have the strength to guide you
and the wisdom to let you guide me.
   -J.M.C.

One day,
my Mommy and Daddy decided
it was time to add another
baby to our family.

My brother was very excited!

The doctors told
my Mommy and Daddy
that they were having
another boy.

Since I was just a
teeny tiny baby
in Mommy's belly,
I could not tell them
how I felt.

My Mommy said that
my favorite color was pink
and my favorite toys
were headbands
and dress up clothes.

My brother thought
that was silly.

My Daddy thought
it was silly too.

But my Mommy told me,
"I love you if you love pink.
I love you if you love blue.
I love you, my sweet baby,
no matter what."

When I was old enough to walk and talk,
I discovered princesses.

Oh, how I just loved everything about princesses!

I loved to sing princess songs and wear princess clothes. I most especially loved to wear sparkly princess high heels.

My brother thought
that was silly.

My Daddy thought
it was silly too.

But my Mommy told me,
"I love you if you are
a handsome prince.
I love you if you are
a beautiful princess.
I love you, my sweet baby,
no matter what."

When I grew old enough to play sports, my Mommy and Daddy signed me up for soccer. But, I did not like soccer. I did not like running or kicking the ball. I especially did not like being outside in the hot sun.

My Mommy said we could try a dance class instead.
I loved the way my feet made clicking sounds on the floor in my tap shoes.
I loved spinning around high up on my tip toes in my ballet shoes.

My brother thought
that was silly.

My Daddy thought
it was silly too.

But my Mommy told me,
"I love you if you are
a soccer star.
I love you if you are
a graceful ballerina.
I love you, my sweet baby,
no matter what."

When I grew older, my Mommy and Daddy would take me shopping for clothes. I loved the clothes with colors and sparkles.

I loved clothes with giant bows and ruffled sleeves. I would ask to buy all these beautiful things instead of clothes like my brother had. Sometimes my Mom would let me get new clothes with bright colors, but sometimes she still made me wear my old clothes. My bright colored clothes made me happy!

My brother thought
that was silly.

My Daddy thought
it was silly too.

But my Mommy told me,
"I love you in your
old clothes.
I love you in your
bright colored clothes.
I love you, my sweet baby,
no matter what."

One day
I told my Mommy and Daddy
that the baby doctor was wrong.
I was not a boy at all.
I was a girl.

My Mommy and Daddy took me to
a special doctor to understand
how I was feeling.
Together, with the special doctor,
my Mommy, Daddy, and I
learned that my body
does not match my brain
or my heart.

After all that learning,
my Mommy and Daddy decided
I can live as my true self,
the way my brain and heart feel.
My Mommy and Daddy said
I could grow my hair long.
They said I could wear
all those beautiful,
sparkly and ruffled clothes
I loved so much.
They even said
I could change my name.

My brother called me,
"Brave."

My Daddy called me,
"Amazing."

Mommy leaned in close and
.sed my head as she whispered,

"I love you if you are a boy.

I love you if you are a girl.

I love you, my sweet baby,

no matter what."

16310081R00018

Made in the USA
Middletown, DE
23 November 2018